SPOTLIGHT ON SPACE SCIENCE

JOURNEY THROUGH THE ASTEROID BELT

MARK DILLARD

New York

Published in 2015 by The Rosen Publishing Group, Inc.
29 East 21st Street, New York, NY 10010

First Edition

Editor: Susan Meyer
Book Design: Kris Everson

Photo Credits: Cover (background), p. 11 ESA/ATG medialab; cover (inset), p. 5 Japanese Aerospace Exploration Agency (JAXA); pp. 6, 7, 14, 18 NASA; pp. 9, 17, 21, 23, 29 NASA/JPL-Caltech; p. 13 Universal History Archive/Contributor/Universal Images Group/Getty Images; p. 15 Dave Williams, NASA; p. 19 NASA, ESA, and Z. Levay (STScI); p. 25 Andrea Danti/Shutterstock.com; p. 27 NASA/JPL-Caltech/UMD.

Library of Congress Cataloging-in-Publication Data

Dillard, Mark.
Journey through the asteroid belt / by Mark Dillard.
p. cm. — (Spotlight on space science)
Includes index.
ISBN 978-1-4994-0367-1 (pbk.)
ISBN 978-1-4994-0396-1 (6-pack)
ISBN 978-1-4994-0410-4 (library binding)
1. Asteroids — Juvenile literature. 2. Asteroid belt — Juvenile literature. I. Title.
QB651.D55 2015
523.44—d23

Manufactured in the United States of America

CPSIA Compliance Information: Batch #CW15PK: For Further Information contact Rosen Publishing, New York, New York at 1-800-237-9932

CONTENTS

COLLISION COURSE WITH EARTH?

CHAPTER 1

A group of scientists and military officers are arguing in the White House. An asteroid the size of Texas is just days from colliding with Earth, and no one knows what to do.

Suddenly, a scruffy geek bursts into the room.

He has made some mathematical calculations and has a plan that will save the world from disaster!

This may be an exciting plot for a movie, but could Earth one day collide with a giant asteroid? **Astronomers** estimate that millions of asteroids may be **orbiting** our Sun. So how did they get there, what do we know about them, and could one of them be heading our way any time soon?

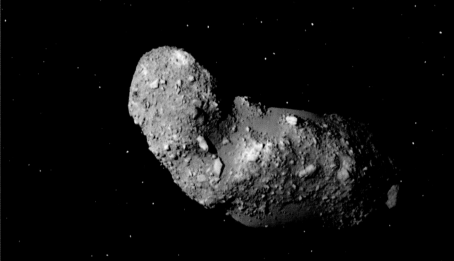

The asteroid Itokawa has a bumpy exterior because it is likely made up of rocky debris that has built up over time.

ASTEROIDS BIG AND SMALL

CHAPTER 2

Asteroids are Earth's rocky space neighbors. Most are shaped like lumpy potatoes!

Asteroids are made of rocky materials, just like Mercury, Venus, Earth, and Mars. Some also contain metals, such as iron, nickel, and even gold.

the asteroid Eros

Asteroids can be as small as a car, or as large as a mountain. The largest known asteroid, Ceres, has a diameter of 600 miles (966 km)!

Here the asteroid Ceres (center) is seen compared in size to Earth (right), Earth's moon (top center), and the **dwarf planet** Eris (left).

FORMATION OF ASTEROIDS

CHAPTER 3

The millions of asteroids orbiting our Sun were created when our solar system formed about 4.5 billion years ago.

Before the solar system came into being, there was a huge cloud of gas and dust in space. Over time, the cloud collapsed on itself. Most of the gas and dust collected around the center of the cloud, creating a massive ball, or sphere. As the sphere rotated, or turned, in space, a disk formed around the sphere from the remaining gas and dust.

As all this matter rotated, the sphere pulled in more gas and dust, adding to its size, weight, and **gravity**. The pressure of all the material pressing onto the center of the sphere caused the center to get hotter and hotter. Finally, the temperature inside the sphere got so hot that the sphere ignited to become a star—our Sun!

Inside the rotating disk, other masses formed to become the solar system's planets and their moons. Millions of smaller masses did not fuse together to create planets. Rocky chunks close to the Sun became asteroids, while icy chunks away from the Sun became **comets**.

Asteroids form from the leftover gas and dust in the birth of a planetary system.

A ROCKY RING
CHAPTER 4

Asteroids orbit the Sun in many parts of the solar system. Most of them are in a huge area known as the **asteroid belt**.

The asteroid belt is between the orbits of Mars and Jupiter. In this area, millions of asteroids form a vast, donut-shaped ring.

Sometimes asteroids leave the belt. This may happen when an asteroid is nudged out of its orbit by the powerful gravity of Jupiter, the largest planet in the solar system. Such an asteroid might even end up in an orbit closer to Earth.

Sometimes when asteroids hit each other, they may break up into pieces. The orbits of these pieces, called **meteoroids**, might cross Earth's orbit. They may even enter Earth's atmosphere as fiery **meteors**, which we call shooting stars!

Larger meteoroids that do not burn up in the atmosphere may land on Earth as **meteorites.**

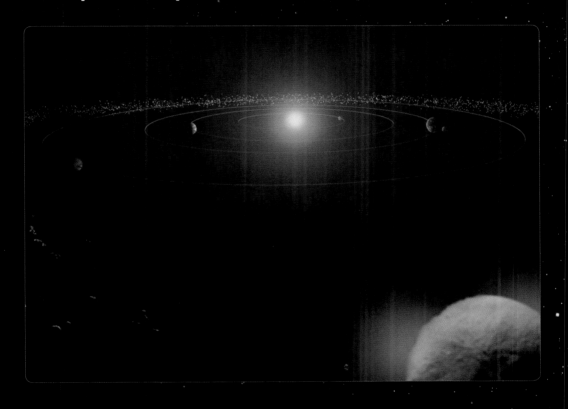

This drawing shows the asteroid belt surrounding our solar system. In the foreground is Ceres, the largest object in the asteroid belt.

ASTEROID OR PLANET?

CHAPTER 5

On January 1, 1801, an Italian astronomer named Giuseppe Piazzi discovered an object orbiting the Sun. Piazzi thought he had seen a new planet through his telescope. In fact, he had found Ceres, the first asteroid to be discovered!

Astronomers soon discovered more of these rocky bodies that acted like planets, but were much smaller. Today, over 500,000 asteroids have been found and studied.

In 2006, a group of astronomers called the International Astronomical Union created a new category for space objects that look and act like planets, but are much smaller. Objects in this new category would be known as dwarf planets. Since its discovery in 1930, Pluto had been defined as a planet. In 2006, it was redefined as a dwarf planet. In that same year, Ceres, the biggest of all the asteroids, was also defined as a dwarf planet.

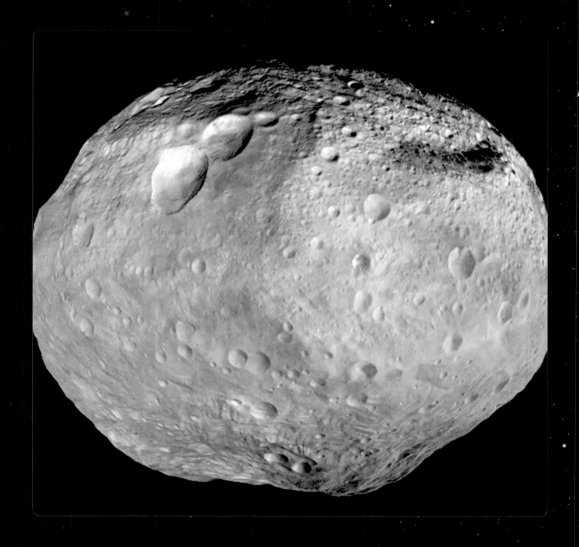

Vesta is one of the largest asteroids in our solar system. Vesta alone makes up 9 percent of the total mass of the asteroid belt.

STUDYING ASTEROIDS

CHAPTER 6

Until the 1990s, astronomers were only able to study asteroids from Earth using telescopes. In 1991, however, the NASA spacecraft *Galileo* took the first-ever close-up photographs of an asteroid!

On its way to Jupiter, *Galileo* photographed the asteroids Gaspra and Ida. *Galileo* also discovered that Ida had its own moon, which was named Dactyl.

In 1996, NASA launched the first-ever space mission designed especially to visit an asteroid. The *NEAR* (*Near Earth Asteroid Rendezvous*) *Shoemaker* spacecraft made a flyby of asteroid Mathilde. Then, in 2000, it went into orbit around Eros. *NEAR*

The rocket carrying *NEAR Shoemaker* blasts off on February 17, 1996.

Shoemaker transmitted data about and close-up images of Eros back to Earth.

On February 12, 2001, *NEAR Shoemaker* touched down on the surface of Eros. Later that month, it shut down its transmissions forever. Eros and its man-made hitchhiker might now be flying through space together for billions of years!

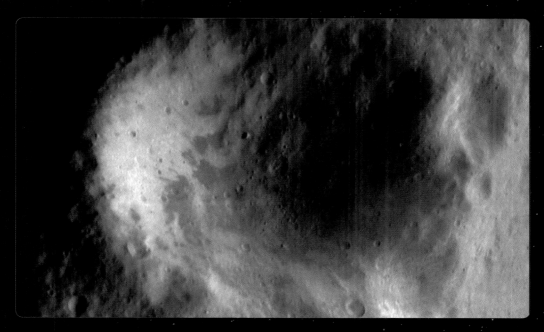

This photo shows Psyche, a large crater on the asteroid Eros. It is a composite image of a number of photos taken by NEAR Shoemaker in 2000.

THE *DAWN* MISSION
CHAPTER 7

On September 27, 2007, NASA launched the *Dawn* mission. The spacecraft *Dawn* was to travel into the solar system beyond Mars to study and compare Ceres and Vesta, two of the largest bodies in the asteroid belt.

Dawn reached Vesta in July 2011. It was a journey of four years and 1.8 billion miles (2.9 billion km)! Phase two of the *Dawn* mission is to travel another 990 million miles (1.6 billion km) to enter Ceres' orbit in 2015.

Vesta is a dry, rocky body that is similar to Earth and the other planets of the inner solar system. Ceres, however, seems closer in its makeup to icy bodies in the farthest reaches of the solar system. The *Dawn* mission's objective is to learn more about how these two very different asteroids formed, and maybe unlock some of the secrets of how our solar system was formed.

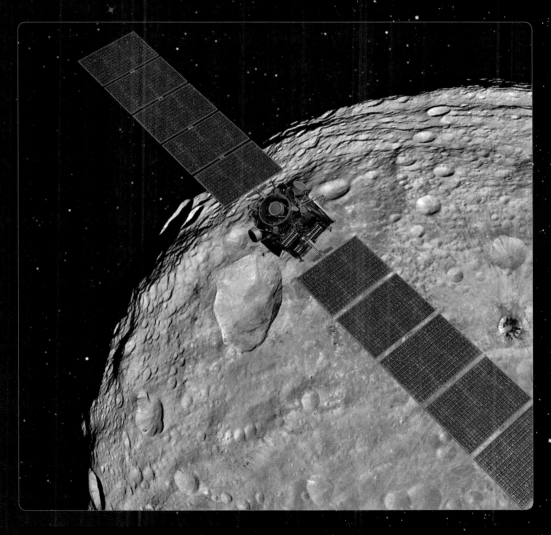

Dawn orbited the asteroid Vesta for nearly 14 months, collecting photos and mapping the giant asteroid's surface.

CRATER-COVERED VESTA

Vesta was discovered by German astronomer Heinrich Wilhelm Olbers on March 29, 1807. It was the fourth asteroid to be discovered, so it is officially named "4 Vesta."

The asteroid's surface is made from basaltic rock. This rock was once **lava** that oozed from the hot inside of the asteroid, just as lava pours from a volcano on Earth and then hardens.

On the south pole of Vesta there is a giant crater 285 miles (459 km) across and 8 miles (13 km) deep. At some time in its history, Vesta collided with another space body and a huge chunk of the asteroid broke off, leaving

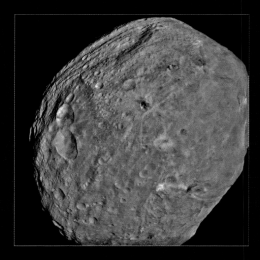

This photograph of Vesta was taken by *Dawn* from a distance of 3,231 miles (5,200 km) away.

behind the crater. Scientists believe that pieces of Vesta as small as grains of sand and as large as mountains were hurled out into the solar system!

Vesta

Earth's moon

500 miles
805 kilometers

Vesta's diameter is approximately 15 percent of our Earth's moon.

UP CLOSE WITH CERES

CHAPTER 9

Ceres, which is also considered a dwarf planet, was the first asteroid to be discovered because it was the easiest to see from Earth! If Ceres' diameter of about 600 miles (966 km) is hard to imagine, just think of it as being almost as far across as the width of Texas!

Ceres has a central core of hard material, a mantle, and an outer crust. Scientists believe that the mantle, which is 62 miles (100 km) thick, is made of ice. If this is correct, it would mean that Ceres contains more freshwater than Earth!

Ceres may also have ice at its north and south poles—just like Earth.

As of 2014, the Dawn probe *that studied the asteroid Vesta is on its way to study Ceres.*

NEAR-EARTH OBJECTS

CHAPTER 10

In 1990, astronomers knew of 182 Near-Earth Objects (NEOs). Today, they have identified and are watching thousands.

An NEO is an asteroid or comet that comes close to Earth's path around the Sun. For such objects, "close" is within 28 million miles (45 million km). That might seem like a huge distance, but compared with the vastness of space, it's not very far at all.

Every day, Earth is hit by a lot of dust and tiny particles from space, but how often does Earth collide with something seriously large?

Scientists estimate that an asteroid or comet about the size of a football field collides with Earth every few hundred years.

Once every few million years, something heads for our planet that has the potential to end all life on Earth!

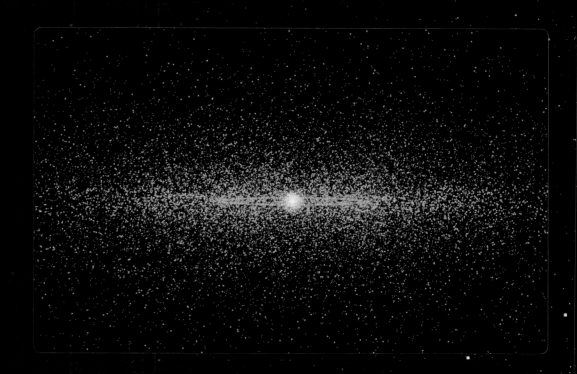

In this diagram, the dots represent near-Earth asteroids that scientists believe exist. The green line shows Earth's orbit.

EXTINCTION OF THE DINOSAURS

CHAPTER 11

In the late 1970s, scientists discovered a huge crater near the town of Chicxulub on the Yucatan Peninsula, in Mexico. The crater is evidence that at some point in our planet's history, something had collided with Earth—something big. Very big!

Over millions of years, the crater had become hidden under layers of rock and soil, but scientists were able to collect data to prove its existence.

Over time, scientists concluded that an asteroid or comet at least 6 miles (9.7 km) wide had collided with Earth about 65 million years ago. The result of this devastating event was the extinction of up to 70 percent of the **species** on Earth—including the dinosaurs!

The collision may have caused huge tidal waves and earthquakes and thrown up vast clouds of incredibly hot ash and steam that covered the skies across the planet.

A large asteroid colliding with our planet destroyed much of the life on Earth 65 million years ago.

With thousands of known Near-Earth Objects in orbits close to our planet, what's being done to keep track of these rocky neighbors, and how do we know when a new hazard moves into our space neighborhood?

NASA and other space organizations are constantly watching the skies for new objects that have moved from elsewhere in the solar system and are now orbiting close to Earth.

When a new NEO is discovered, its orbit is plotted into the future to enable scientists to see if the object will ever be on a collision course with Earth.

So what could be done if a large NEO was heading for Earth? A spacecraft could be flown into the asteroid to knock it off course. A robotic craft known as a "gravity tractor" could also be sent to cruise alongside the asteroid. The craft's gravity would pull the asteroid off course so that it missed Earth.

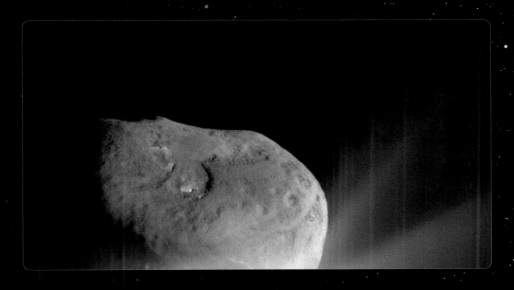

This photo shows the asteroid Tempel 1 one minute after the Deep Impact spacecraft intentionally crashed into it.

KEEPING EARTH SAFE

CHAPTER 13

On November 8, 2011, an asteroid the size of an aircraft carrier made its closest approach to Earth in 200 years.

The asteroid, called 2005 YU55, was just 201,700 miles (324,600 km) from Earth! It was the largest Near-Earth Object to come this close to Earth in about 30 years. YU55 is just one of thousands of Near-Earth Objects that scientists continue to track. By studying them and understanding their orbits, they can rule out any potential danger to our planet.

At this moment in time, thanks to astronomers and monitoring systems around the world, we can be sure that there is no threat of Earth colliding with any of the known Near-Earth Objects for at least the next 100 years.

For now, our little place in the solar system is safe. The only giant asteroids heading for Earth are the ones in the movies!

The Wide-field Infrared Survey Explorer, or WISE, *orbits the Earth and surveys NEOs in our solar system. Its mission lasted from 2009 to 2011, and it started a new mission to continue its work in 2013.*

GLOSSARY

asteroid belt: The region between Mars and Jupiter that contains millions of asteroids in a donut-shaped ring.

astronomer: A person who studies space objects.

comet: A space object made of ice and dust with a tail that points away from the Sun.

dwarf planet: A space object that looks and acts like a planet, but is much smaller.

gravity: The force that pulls on an object toward the center of another object that has mass.

lava: Melted rock that comes out of a volcano.

meteor: A streak of light in the night sky produced by a piece of matter from space burning up in Earth's atmosphere; also referred to as a shooting star.

meteorite: A piece of matter from space that passes through Earth's atmosphere and strikes the ground.

meteoroid: A small piece of an asteroid that has broken off from the main mass.

orbit: To move around an object along a curved path; also, the curved path of a space object around a star, planet, or moon.

species: A group of plants or animals that are all the same kind.

FOR MORE INFORMATION

BOOKS

Aguilar, David A. *Space Encyclopedia: A Tour of Our Solar System and Beyond.* Washington, D.C.: National Geographic, 2013.

Chiger, Arielle, and Adrienne Houk Maley. *20 Fun Facts About Asteroids and Comets.* New York, NY: Gareth Stevens Publishing, 2015.

Jackson, Tom. *Our Solar System: A Nonfiction Companion to the Original Magic School Bus Series.* New York, NY: Scholastic, 2014.

WEBSITES

Due to the changing nature of Internet links, PowerKids Press has developed an online list of websites related to the subject of this book. This site is updated regularly. Please use this link to access the list: www.powerkidslinks.com/soss/aster

INDEX